U.S. Immigration Today

Antonio Sacre, M.A.

Reader Consultants

Brian Allman, M.A.
Classroom Teacher, West Virginia

Cheryl Norman Lane, M.A.Ed.
Classroom Teacher, California

iCivics Consultants

Emma Humphries, Ph.D.
Chief Education Officer

Taylor Davis, M.T.
Director of Curriculum and Content

Natacha Scott, MAT
Director of Educator Engagement

Publishing Credits

Rachelle Cracchiolo, M.S.Ed., *Publisher*
Emily R. Smith, M.A.Ed., *VP of Content Development*
Véronique Bos, *Creative Director*
Dona Herweck Rice, *Senior Content Manager*
Dani Neiley, *Associate Editor*
Fabiola Sepulveda, *Series Designer*

Image Credits: p11 Shutterstock/Luciano Mortula - LGM; p12 iStock/Sean
Pavone; p13 iStock/AndyParker72; p15 Alamy/Jerome Cid; p16 Hans Dahl
(1849-1937); p19 bottom Library of Congress [LC-DIG-ds-14198]; p20 Shutterstock/
Jazzmany; p21 top Library of Congress [LC-USZ62-60242]; p22 Shutterstock/David
A Litman; p26 Alamy/Jeffrey Isaac Greenberg 5+; all other images from iStock and/or
Shutterstock

Library of Congress Cataloging-in-Publication Data

Names: Sacre, Antonio, 1968- author. | iCivics (Organization)
Title: U.S. immigration today / Antonio Sacre.
Other titles: United States immigration today
Description: Huntington Beach, CA : Teacher Created Materials, 2022. |
  "iCivics"--Cover. | Audience: Grades 4-6 | Summary: "The United States
  is one of the most diverse countries in the world. It is a place where
  people from virtually every other country have chosen to live. How did
  they get there? Why do they go? What are the challenges when they get
  there, and what are the benefits?"-- Provided by publisher.
Identifiers: LCCN 2021054820 (print) | LCCN 2021054821 (ebook) | ISBN
  9781087615509 (paperback) | ISBN 9781087630618 (ebook)
Subjects: LCSH: United States--Emigration and immigration--Juvenile
  literature. | Immigrants--United States--Juvenile literature.
Classification: LCC JV6465 .S24 2022 (print) | LCC JV6465 (ebook) | DDC
  325.73--dc23/eng/20211206
LC record available at https://lccn.loc.gov/2021054820
LC ebook record available at https://lccn.loc.gov/2021054821

5482 Argosy Avenue
Huntington Beach, CA 92649
www.tcmpub.com

ISBN 978-1-0876-1550-9

Table of Contents

On the Move

Let's say you live in a city in the United States. If your mother were offered her dream job in another city in the United States, and it made sense for your family, would you all be allowed to move to that city so she could work at that job? Of course.

Or let's say your family got tired of the cold winters of the Northeast or they were fed up with the desert heat of the Southwest. Are you allowed to move to a different part of the country? Certainly.

What happens if your family always wanted to live **abroad**, maybe in France, Australia, or South Africa? Are you allowed to move there? In most cases, the answer is yes, but it is more complicated. Your family members will need **passports** and **visas**. There might be limits on what you can do, how long you can stay, whether you can work, and so on.

What if you were born and live in another country and your family wants to come to the United States to live and work? Can you do it? The answer is usually yes, but it is even more complicated.

Why people **immigrate** and how they immigrate are complicated topics. Looking at some of the history of immigration and what immigration today involves are good ways to help understand these topics.

Jump into Fiction

Monarch Migration

Enrique stood at home plate on the ball field and stared at his teacher. Mrs. DeHart stood in the middle of a dirt circle. She bounced the small, red rubber ball and yelled, "Are you ready?"

His friend Silvana yelled, "Enrique, do it just like on the soccer field. When it comes to you, blast it with that ridiculous power shot you have! Just pretend the net is way, way, way, way out there."

Enrique smiled, gave her a nod, and then turned his attention to the teacher. "I am ready to score a goal!"

Silvana laughed and said, "It's called a home run, Enrique, not a goal. Just stay focused."

Enrique bounced up and down on his toes and replied, "I am ready to score a home run!"

Mrs. DeHart bent her knees and pulled the ball back but abruptly stopped and stared into the sky, exclaiming in wonder, "They're here!"

All the kids on the ball field turned their eyes toward the sky. Everywhere they looked, clouds of beautiful monarch butterflies scattered and flew, settling in the trees in the city park just beyond their school.

The excited children chased the butterflies, while Silvana stood completely still, waiting for a monarch to alight on her outstretched limbs. Soon, both her arms teemed with butterflies, their colorful wings pulsing as they rested.

Enrique carefully walked toward Silvana and smiled. "They don't usually land on people like that."

"Yeah, I'm kind of a butterfly whisperer," she breathed. "They come from near my hometown in Mexico, flying thousands of miles here to Kansas."

"Why have they migrated so far?" Enrique wondered out loud.

Silvana knew the answer. "The food the baby monarchs need doesn't grow in Mexico at this time of year, so they journey here for the summer. But the winter is too cold for them here, so they will return to Mexico then. They fly back and forth, doing what they need to do to survive."

"How do you know so much about them?" Enrique asked.

"My parents work as scientists at the Monarch Butterfly Biosphere Reserve in Mexico, and we came here so they could study them," Silvana told him.

"I'm glad you immigrated here, just like these butterflies! Do you miss your home?" Enrique asked her.

"I miss my grandparents and my friends but feel lucky to have met you," Silvana said with a smile.

Just then, Mrs. DeHart yelled, "Play ball!" and it was back to the game.

Back to Nonfiction

Why Come to the United States?

What are some reasons people come to the United States? The vast majority of people come to the United States each year as **tourists** who want to visit one of the world's amazing countries. America is a top-ten travel spot for many people around the world. People love the views. They visit the Grand Canyon in Arizona. They admire glaciers in Alaska. They visit Florida's beaches.

America is one of the most diverse countries in the world. There is much to see and do.

Many people come to the United States to work or to study. A large number of people are visitors on business. There are major centers of **commerce** and entertainment all over the country. People may work for internet companies in California. They may work in banks in New York City. They may work in hospitals in Ohio. They may work on farms in Iowa. They may work in restaurants or hotels all over. Many top colleges are in the United States, and students come from around the world to study there.

Think and Talk

What challenges might a person face in moving to a new country?

The Most Visited Place
in the World Is . . .

Times Square in New York City is the most visited place in the United States and the world. Over 40 million people visit it each year! They come to see the electronic billboards, to eat at famous restaurants, or to watch Broadway shows.

Families

Throughout history, people have grouped together in families and communities. It is human instinct and the most common way of living. So, when family members live far away, people naturally want to live near them. To reunite their families is one of the biggest reasons why people immigrate to the United States. They move to the country because other family members already live there. They want to keep their families together.

It is also very common for **immigrants** to move to communities of people who are from their home countries. In this way, they can live where some things are familiar to them, such as the food in restaurants and markets, the common music heard, and the language. Places called "Little Italy," "Little Havana," "Chinatown," and so on are common in major cities around the United States for this reason. It is normal to want to be near what a person knows and loves.

There are many others reasons why people immigrate, such as trouble in their home countries and work opportunities. But being with their families is the most common reason.

Oldest Community

St. Augustine in Florida is the oldest European settlement in the United States. It was founded about 450 years ago by Spanish immigrants.

Chinatown in
New York City

A History of Immigration

Immigration is nothing new. People have moved from one place to another for a long time. Here is some of that history. Learning about it can help to understand some of today's immigration.

Early Human Migrants

The earliest humans moved to find more food or to escape changing climates. Huge glaciers in the last Ice Age lowered sea levels and exposed more land, making it easier for early humans to find better places to live.

Early humans formed communities and, as their numbers grew, expanded into other areas. Often, there were other groups already living there. Sometimes, they would join together to form bigger communities. Each influenced the other in this group. Or there would be war between these people. Many would flee these war-torn areas to other safer places.

This painting is an artist's idea of early human migration.

Sadly, there are many examples through history of communities and countries entering another area and doing great harm to the people living there. This is called **persecution**. Persecution continues today. It takes many forms. Some people are not allowed to practice their religions. Some are not allowed to be educated. Some are forced to live in terrible conditions. Millions have been killed. People try to fight this persecution. Often, they immigrate to safer places and hope to return to their home countries one day.

People who flee their home countries because of troubles there are known as *refugees*.

A Diverse Country

The United Nations says that the country with the most foreign-born people in the world is the United States. It has five times more foreign-born people than the next country on the list. The Census Bureau reports there are over 350 languages spoken in the country.

Waves of Immigration

People have lived in North America for thousands of years. American Indians lived all over the continent. In the 1500s, people started coming to North America from other continents. Since then, historians have identified at least four major waves of immigration to the continent over time.

The first wave was the English settlers. Many of them hoped to practice religion the way they wanted. Spain, Portugal, and France **colonized** other parts of the continent at the same time. The English settlers gained freedom and formed the United States. Many Africans were forced into slavery and taken to the United States. Most American Indians were killed or forced to live on **reservations**. Many of them still live on those lands.

First European in North America

Many people think the first person from Europe in the Americas was Christopher Columbus. But there is evidence that the great Norse explorer Leif Erikkson led the first journey to North America nearly 500 years earlier. A team of experts found items of Viking origin in Canada. These pieces date to around the year 1000.

More than 12 million immigrants came through this main building on Ellis Island, which opened in 1892.

The second wave came in the 1800s. People came from Germany and other parts of Europe. Many of these people worked to build the major cities that stand today. They also brought their farming skills to the Great Plains of the Midwest.

The third wave was in the late 1800s and early 1900s. Many people from Asia moved to the United States. They did much of the work to build the country's railroads, among other contributions.

A fourth wave started in the 1970s. This was a wave of Spanish-speaking people from around the Americas. Work opportunities and rejoining family members were major reasons for this wave.

Ever-Changing Policy

When the colonists fought for independence from England, they wrote the **Declaration of Independence**. In it, they said they wanted to form a new nation where people had certain rights. These rights included the right to choose how and where to live. They wanted freedom of religion and a say in who runs their government. This type of government is a **democracy**.

Early immigration policy encouraged people to come to the United States. There were reasons for this. The government needed people to build the country. Few restrictions were placed on immigration.

The British surrender to end the fight for independence.

Officials examine Japanese immigrants traveling by ship in 1931.

As the United States grew in size, some people began to ask the government to restrict immigration. They wanted to limit who came to the country. The government changed its policy to make it harder to immigrate. Immigrants had to be able to read and write. They could not be very poor. They could not have committed a crime. And they could not come from **communist** countries.

THE AMERICANESE WALL, AS CONGRESSMAN BURNETT WOULD BUILD IT.

UNCLE SAM: You're welcome in—if you can climb it!

This cartoon points out one of the challenges that faced immigrants at one time.

The U.S. government had to figure out ways to handle immigration. Immigrants are important to the life and growth of the United States. But guidelines for immigration are needed, too. Immigration can be a balancing act for the good of the people and the country. To help make policy and develop the best practices for the country, the government founded the U.S. Office of Immigration in 1891. In 1906, it was re-formed as the U.S. Bureau of Immigration. In 1933, it became the U.S. Immigration and Naturalization Service. This organization was responsible for the immigration process and the patrol of U.S. borders. It was the nation's immigration agency for 70 years.

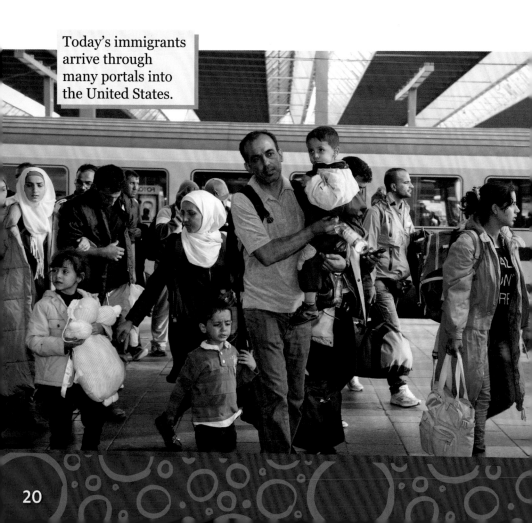

Today's immigrants arrive through many portals into the United States.

Famous Immigrants

Immigrants are part of American culture. They may
be rock stars, athletes, business giants, and more.
Famous immigrants include Albert Einstein, who fled
Nazi Germany. Dikembe Mutombo, a basketball
Hall-of-Famer, was born in the Democratic Republic
of Congo. Justin Bieber, a popstar from Canada,
moved to the United States for his music career.

In 2003, the government reorganized its approach to
immigration once again. It founded the U.S. Citizenship
and Immigration Services (USCIS). There are many issues
the USCIS considers. The way the government handles the
opportunities and challenges of immigration is its *policy*. The
policy looks at many things. How many people can come into
the country? Where can they live? What do they do when
they arrive? Is there space for all immigrants? These are just
some of the things for which policies are made.

Recently, immigration policy has shifted again. Some businesses have a hard time finding workers to do some kinds of work. They want to hire immigrants with the skills they need. For example, farmers needed workers to harvest crops. They pushed for immigrants to be allowed to come and do this work. Businesses asked for more people with special technology skills to come as well.

Immigrants work hard on this farm to harvest crops.

Immigration policy will continue to change as long as immigrants wish to come to the United States. Because it is a nation built on immigration, it is likely that there will always be policies to be made and adjusted. As in the past, the policies of the future will be set to meet the needs of the time.

First Jobs

After moving to the United States, some immigrants find work in labor-intensive fields. These jobs include construction, farming, and cleaning. Many taxi drivers come from other countries, too.

Visas

Immigration to the United States is a legal process. If a person has made the decision to immigrate, there are things they need to know about how it is done.

If you are from another country and want to vacation in the United States, the process is simple. For many countries, you simply show a passport. If you are visiting for work or if you want to study in the United States, you will need a visa. There are visas for work, study, and more. These types of visas are called *nonimmigrant visas,* or *temporary visas.* People go to the United States **Embassy** in their home country to apply for these visas.

Visitors are allowed to stay as tourists for a short time without visas. But if they stay more than 90 days, they are in the country illegally. When a person wants to live in the United States permanently, they need to apply for an immigrant visa, also called a *permanent visa*. People often call this type of visa a *Green Card*. There is an application and a fee to apply for it. Someone might get a Green Card to join a family member already living in the United States or because they have been offered a job in America.

Embassies Almost Everywhere

The United States has embassies in over 160 countries around the world. There are over 170 foreign embassies in the United States, most of them in Washington, DC.

Borders and Customs

All countries in the world want to have their say in who comes into their countries and for how long. They also want to know what items people bring into and out of their countries. Each country has its own rules. To enter or leave the United States, a person must cross the country's borders. If you are not a citizen of the United States, you need special permission to do this.

A **customs** agent welcomes visitors into the United States.

When people come into the United States on airplanes, they cross a border as well. When they land, they go through customs. People at gates check passports. They stamp the passports to say visitors are allowed to enter. They check the travelers' luggage to make sure there are no items that could cause damage. For example, some plants from other countries may have insects that could harm farms in the United States.

The U.S. government wants people to visit the country. When they come, they add to the economy. They enhance American life as well. But the government wants to be sure visitors follow its rules for proper entry.

U.S. Borders

The contiguous United States shares its borders with Canada to the north, Mexico and the Gulf of Mexico to the south, the Atlantic Ocean to the east, and the Pacific Ocean to the west.

For the Good of All

The monarch butterfly is a symbol of migration. It is a beautiful and delicate thing. It moves because it has to. It moves because of conditions that it cannot control and did not create.

This is true for many immigrants as well. Some people leave their home countries because they feel they have to. Others want to create a better life for themselves and their families. Many immigrants simply hope to reunite with their loved ones or may be looking for change or adventure that a new job offers in a new place.

Some people are not happy about immigration policy in the United States. When people in a democracy are not happy, they have the power to change it. Abraham Lincoln said the nation is a "government of the people, by the people, for the people." People make their voices heard. They can contact their elected leaders. They can also join in marches or protests to make their opinions known.

The United States has changed its mind about many things over time. It has even changed its Constitution. It has changed its policies on many issues.

Many people struggle with the idea of immigration. Some people think the United States needs stronger laws. Others believe the current laws are unfair and need to change. If history is any indication, the people of the United States will find a way to do what's best for the country. It may not be perfect. People on all sides of an issue must compromise. But just as the United States has always done, it will keep working to make better policies for the good of all.

Glossary

abroad—in or to a foreign country

colonized—took control of an area and sent people to live there

commerce—activities that relate to the buying and selling of goods and services

communist—related to a person or country who supports a system where all property is owned by the whole public

customs—a place at a border crossing where officials check incoming goods and baggage

Declaration of Independence—a decree in which American colonists announced their separation from Britain, in 1776

democracy—a form of government in which citizens elect their leaders by voting

embassy—a group of people who work under an ambassador and represent their country in a foreign country, often where visas are granted to visit that country

immigrants—people who come to live permanently in another country

immigrate—to leave one's home country to live somewhere else

passports—official documents issued by governments that show people's identities and citizenship and let them travel to and from foreign countries

persecution—hostility and ill-treatment, especially because of a person's race or religion

reservations—areas of land in the United States that are kept separate as a place for American Indians to live

tourists—people who travel places temporarily for pleasure

visas—documents that allow people to enter, leave, or stay in a country for a period of time

Index

Civics in Action

Newly arrived immigrants have many needs. They may not speak English fluently. They do not know the area well. They need housing, food, schools, and all the basic things in life. You can aid newly arrived immigrants in your area.

1. Brainstorm items and information they may need.

2. Research and gather those items and information into a welcome kit.

3. Make a plan to distribute the kits.

4. Distribute them!